THE HEART OF THE BLESSED (PART 2)

DHARMAMBAL S, MUKUND IYER AND KSHITIJA IYER

Made with ♥ on the Notion Press Platform
www.notionpress.com

Dear Readers,

Part 1 of this book is also available on Notionpress.com.

It would be really encouraging if you check that out and read it!

Thank you for the support!

Contents

Contents

1. LIFE

Things you don't choose
Makes you who you are.
The city you live in,
The neighbors you have
The family The pride,
People carry.
Though not accomplished,
But it still likes bodies
Wrapped around souls.
Can't one be calm,
Like A sheep among wolves,
Can't one be wise
Like A serpent.
And still, be innocent
Like A dove?

2. LAW

Natural law that innate sense of justice
Exist in each one of us
Reminding us of its importance
To prioritize what is right over the ruler,
What is right over the law?
Laws change
What is right will always be right.

3. FREEDOM

Absolute freedom simply scares you
Your hate is not what others succeed in
Your hate is a cause of you not doing so
Hate aroused from failure
Failure to destruction
Incredible success of others
If it could fill in happiness
Not sure how to fill in you
But for the others
Who succeeds in their
Endeavor
Freedom from hate, jealousy, revenge
Freedom from malicious thoughts
Freedom to build
A world a better world
You are truly free.

4. WOMAN IN ME

Tears from eyes flow
Pains inflow as it grows
Spreads through like mold
Is it for the woman in me?
Wades through troubled times
With head held high
With a smile on the face
The ember that blazes forever
Treading ahead ahead
For a better a better the best of
In whatever I do to achieve.
I achieved it.

5. CONFLICTS

A female protagonist
Living in a big house
That could be seen
Only on an elite magazine cover.
Just wakes up to view
A scenario made just for her.
Spending her luxury time
No long lines to stand
No time cards to punch
Cooking pansies in my spare time
What she does is
For nothing to be served
Wearing the best of clothing
As soft as just-born lambs
Spending weekends
Massaging to softening
Reading every first-edition
At its publishing.
SO WHAT IS THE CONFLICT?
Taken advantage of
Making one feel less
For all the hard work.

WORK THE ONE THING
ONE CAN COUNT ON
FOR EVERYTHING ELSE IS FRAGILE.

6. MEMORIES

Have I forgotten?
This is the question that
lingers in my mind.
Moving about your daily chores
Smiling, laughing,
Shouting, fighting!
Have I been thought
Seeing parents curdling their children.
Seeing youngsters walking along
Holding their elders' hands
Protecting entangled fingers
Expressing their care
Fondling, loving,
Sharing, Bearing!
As I am breathing in Memories
Leading the way
Led by you.
As I am breathing out the stress
Paving the path for
Generations to come
As you bore the torch
So shall I

With

Blessing showering

By you and your Almighty.

7. FEARS

We must overcome our fears
Sooner or later.
Living with them
Not forgetting helps
Helps to understand
Who you are?
Two ways to see it or
Two ways to live it?
Things that keep us together

8. LOVE

Love is beautiful
But it is not true.
Love is but a word.
For thousands of
different things,
possessive love
destructive love
Love that destroys you
Consider carefully
Too much showered upon
Can consume
Too much attracted towards
Can lead to wrong ones.
Emotional, passionate
Without much
Under one's control
Will lead into the abyss.

9. MEANING OF LIFE

Go on picnics.
Visit your maternal and paternal home.
Enjoy with your siblings
Cook and relish the food you enjoyed
In the serene and carefree life.
Have fun creating memories.
Busy may be schedules
Collecting memories
For the retired life
Seek the meaning of life
Bonding to strengthen
Leaving behind
Bad memories
Financial status/
For humane
Brought up
Respecting the manufacturer's guidance
A Pride to carry.

10. DESIRE

Desire for comfort
Desire for more
Not knowing what is in store.
Yearning for milk
A desire for flavored rises.
Thirst for water
Sufficed by sweetened drinks.
Craves for hot drinks
A desire for healthy drinks thrives.
Showered with love
Seeks more and more.
Grows as lust
Desire to burn in lust.
Awaits for Variety
Timeless sense arose
Heedless to true love though.
Desire burns one out
Partner seeking
Blessed is life
True love
Wings up
Flies past

Hurdles, troubles, quibbles
Affection subdues
Stress, pain, sorrow.
Shadowing dark past
Clouding jarring truth
Drizzling off the past
Barring the harsh truth
Life moves on
Resolving
Rejoicing
Blessed to have crossed the crossroads.
Still desire burns
Desires for peaceful exit.
Desire....desire......desire....
Keeps you burning
Keep it burning
Burning till you REST.

11. INTELLIGENCE

Earning, living, eating, reproducing,
Dying one day.
What a small insect could do,
Living, eating, reproducing,
Dying one day.
Is what a human does
But what a creature could do
With a big fuss,
Doing anything and everything,
But still struggling
With what they are doing
But ever struggling
With their brain themselves
Intelligence of theirs
Is what humans's big problem.

12. TONGUE

Handle it right.
It will make you like
It will take your life.
Anger, resentment, hatred,
Are all poisons that
You drink and expect
Somebody Else to die.
You drink poison, you die.
Chemical poison
Never hurts others
But it hurts you.
Abuse from mouth
Belongs from where
It is uttered from.
A bullet hits and hurts
React causes suffering.
Abused in a language unknown
With a smile
Will haunt you
Experience what has
Happen to you
Is determined by you

What the world throws at us
Is not necessarily our choice
But what you make out of it
Is entirely your choice.

13. HOW ONE LIVES

The world that loves us
Hurts us day by day
Knowing death awaits.
Earth Graves our bodies
Masses of human bodies.
It is not how long we live
But it is the way we live.
The day threads of our lives
Snaps without saying goodbye
We are going to meet
To carry or to support each other.
We are born to live
And we live to die.
Death does it care?
The suffering we have gone through
Mistreated were we
We wanted to live
A decade passed through
Without the care or support
By whom the world says so.
Mercy by him showered
As sheltered, fed, pampered

Loved smoothly did a decade

Go by to live happily.

14. ANXIETY

Are you suffering?
Suffering for what
happened!
Happened years ago?
Next, what is going
happen?
Maybe it happens?
Suffering should
either
Make you wise or
wounded!
Decide on the choice
given.
Ticking away life.
More dearer is
the grave.
Carry not the
Suffering.
Like a wound
pinning painting!
Became wiser
faster

Wounded do you
perfer?
For education
has taught.
What can't be corrected
must be endured.

15. CONTROL

Control your

thoughts and emotions.

If you have not learned

Learn to control

your thoughts and emotions.

Knowing not to drive a bike.

Leads to accidents.

If you drive so

unknowingly!

It starts rolling speeds up

Speed leads to fear.

faster it goes

bucks up terror

Learn to drive

speed up

faster it goes

Balanced is the drive.

Learn to control

thoughts and emotions.

Else enmeshed in it

complicated would it be?

Distance oneself

everything clears.
Calm mind
Pure heart
Action of selflessness
Action filled with love
Purity of head
Purity of action
Purity of heart
Discipline your
thoughts and emotions
Discipline in living
Deliberate living
Discipline and practice
Control your
thoughts and emotions.
To lead a peaceful
disease-free life.

16. LIFE PARTNER

Pinning away
As I try to climb
Climb up the valley
Valley in the desert
Deserted dunes
Dunes formed
Over years of togetherness
Togetherness amidst hot or cold
Cold relationship dried
Dried the moist
Moist ashes of the flame
Flame of the bond
Bonded to face
Face ups and downs
Down went the faith
Faith in each other
Others envied us
Us had gone to me
Me entangled in duties
Duties to be done
Done were the responsibilities
Responsibilities not shared

Shared by those who loved
Loved unconditionally
Unconditional love
Love that does not bond with faith
Faith between them had been seized
Seized by the so-called relationships
Relationships for advantages
Advantages one sided
Sided away the bond between
Between the partners bonded by
Unconditional love.

17. MISTAKES

When you commit a mistake
You should fear.
Regret for the same
You swell with pride.
Instead of getting caught
In the whirlpool of fear
Take pride in regretting, repenting,
Filling your heart with
Wondrous happiness dear.
You are a radiant person.
To rise to touch the sky
Extend your roots
Be down to earth humble and grateful.
Silence can bring down
All the good and bad thoughts.
Letting go of these egoistic
Dogmas and concepts.
Mistakes and fears.

18. SINNER

Evil never gets punished
In this dogmatic world.
Retributive justice is
Served randomly
For sins have an end.
If it was him to be crucified
For all our sins,
It is for him to forgive us
For the sins we commit.
Sinners are punished
For the sins committed knowingly
Forgiveness is not rendered.
For angels too are thrown
Into the hell
Pit of Darkness
Until the day of reckoning!

19. MY LIFE

What thou heart is filled?
With joyous memories?
Or tears of sorrow?
I would reply filled with
Joy, love, voracity.
Where am I?
Would you ask?
With supercilious smile
Would I obdurately say
My heart is full of life.
Rapaciousness of yours
Queries "My life or Yours?"
My heart is full of My life!
Walking away blinded
Unaware that you are **MY LIFE.**

20. MY DAY

Morn to raise
Whole day long
To kick the bucket.
Bring rice bowl to the table
Work to the toughest
Not what we are
To work for
Not that we are
Paid upto mark
Still, go on pulling
Enjoying the direful
Cause may not
Be there the next morning.

21. MY OLD FLAME

Loving you was what I knew
For which I have no regrets.
Was only thankful to you
For I learned what love can't be.
Seeing you was what I lost
For my heartbeat never skipped.
Was only thankful to you
For upon a look, it stopped to beat.
Loving you was just an idea
For there was nothing for me to love.
Realizing I never really loved you
For it was just a thought.
Giving all I possess to you
For nothing attached to love.
Signs of which it is what I knew
For what love in truth would be.

22. STAND UP STILL

Want to see me fail?
As you may tread
On me with all your malice?

Want to make me upset?
You may walk
On me with all your hate?

Want to see me broken?
So you may cut through
On me with all your awful grudge?

Still, I stand up upright
Up straight from your malice
Up with shoulders held high
Up with my haughty pride.

Up from the dirty pit pushed into
Up from the pieces broken into
Up from the cuts torn into

Treading past the shame
Grumbling with the rooted pain
Jumping, leaping, swelling, up high.

Leaving behind those dark days
Blessing showered by ancestors
Gifted and tendered
I stand up high.

23. A STUDENT'S CRY

Could have been a cricketer
But was driven/crushed/killed.
The pitch was replaced by physics.
Sound resonations,
High-pitch calculations.

Could have been a painter
But was driven/crushed/killed.
Colors were replaced by Maths.
Operations, subtractions
Brushed off my aspirations.

Could have been a chef
But was driven/crushed/killed
Spices were replaced by chemicals.
Equations dissolving a chef to be a catalyst.

You decided who I
Should be as a parent.
Crushing my dreams
In pursuit of what
You wanted to be.

You guided whom I
Could be as a teacher.
Ceiling my career
In pursuit of what
You could have been.

Could never see beyond
Or even share my dreams
For the blinkers
Protected me from
Distractions
Forbade me from
Conversing
With strangers
Rules bonded me
Within the four walls

Now, you are equipped. Fly!
How do I fly?
Not a word
I gasp at a crowd
Rendering a speech?
If at all
Can't converse friendly

24. MY LIFE MY TERMS

Had many who let you down
Had many unresolved problems
Had many a time tried to please

Let me not walk along those
Let me not untangle those
Let me not try to please.

Poisonous flowing through my veins
Neither did it let me grow
Nor did they let me live

Live in peace
Live for those
Live for the love of oneself.

25. A MESSAGE TO

I did manage to survive
Everything is under control
I did break, not shatter into pieces
Hopes and dreams got derailed

Depressed, welding sorrows
Clouded by confusions
Seeping through was the
Thawing pain seizing down

Learning to sleep with sorrows
Smiling soothing the pains
Rising with head held high
I found my sense of
Profound peace within me.

26. PARTS OF SPEECH

In school I understand,
What is knowledge?
Knowledge is not what you gain,
From books nor
From experiences
Or traveler's log
Or the news channels.
In school, I learn
What is life
VERBS *enhanced*
*By an **ADVERB***
Could only produce
*An **ADJECTIVE** for the*
***NOUN**- teacher. And*
***PRONOUN** - student*
My travel log
Full of experiences
***PREPOSITIONS** connected well by*
CONJUNCTIONS** and **CONNECTORS
Bringing us teachers together
Students on to stage

Unexpected results leaving
Our teachers full of
INTERJECTIONS.

27. PAIN

Life is full of pain
The most important
Entity of human life.
The pain felt by the prick
Given by the thorn.
The pain felt by the burn
Given by the fire.
The pain felt by the cut
Given by the knife.
The pain felt by the bruise
Given by the fall.
The pain felt by the lies
Given by the loved ones.
The pain felt by the neglect
Given by the one whom
You think as your own.
The pain felt by the words
Given the insensitive
Around the world.
The pain helps us gain
The strength to
Wriggle out of pain

Exit to walk back
Into the zone of comfort.
The pain helps us move
Toward the success
May feel the drain
Polish you to shine
Leaving rest to whine.

28. CHILD'S SMILE

You can see the bright sun
Can feel the warmth.
You can listen to the breeze
Can feel the chill.
You can see the rainfall
Can feel the freeze.
You can see the child's eye
Can expect some naughtiness.
You can see the child's face
Can sense his traits.
You can see the child's stride
Can imagine his aim.
You can see the child's smile
Can find how happy he is!

29. TRIBUTE TO MY STUDENTS

CHILDREN
I planted a sapling
In my garden
Tended it watered it
Patted it and smoothed it.

Expecting it to bloom
It grew but not tall
It grew but did not shine
It grew but did not bloom.

The weeds around
Hindered it stumbled it
Frightened it crumpled it
Crushed it destroyed it.

My folds could never
Help it bloom.
Every support at its fall
Stiffened its wings

It failed to fly.

Uproot? Yes! Replantation
Strengthened its wings.
Alone it struggled
To fly high
To swim deep
To fight the deadly
To stand alone, apart
To speak for its right
To set oneself on a path
To progress.

Bloom my child
Shine my child
Grow my child.

Let my lamp light dimly
Lit for you.
Let every success of yours
Brighten it.
Let every step forward
Make it glow.
Glow glow glow until
It sets to sparkle
It's the world around us.

30. WILD IMAGINATION

Wild imagination
Greater than a bird's flight
In this wide blue sky.

Soar up high as an eagle
In search of new spheres
Raise to new heights.

Freedom from fears
Freedom from tears
Freedom to love
Freedom to live.

A life full of ups and downs
Full of thorns and petals
Full of hot and cool moments
Full of bright colors too.

Freedom to share
Freedom to bare

Freedom to care
Freedom to be cared for.

Strong determination
Powerful than a jaguar's race
In this deep wide world.
Discovering the past
Refreshing the present
Strengthening self to achieve success.

31. MY CHILD (foot by foot)

I hold your hands
For you to take a step
For you to tread ahead
For you to stand straight
For you to hold your head high.

Step By Step
We walked together.

For you to gather strength
For you to gain confidence
For you fathom a future bright.
For you to stand apart upright.

Higher the flight
Rose to heights

For you to shine
For you to soothe the pain

For you to gain

For you to reign.

• 46 •

32. AGING

Seeing flowers bloom
The fragrance of the bloom
Forces away the gloom
Bring tiny tots out of the room.

Gathering of the dark clouds
Pattering of the raindrops
Blabbering of babies
Wobbling kids.

Noisy classrooms
Dusty playgrounds
Melodies in the music rooms
Smelly lab rooms.

Crowy showrooms
Grizzly bar rooms
Crazy dance rooms
Smoky bedrooms.

Busy office hours
Rush at shops

Share of kitchen

That's what partners are for.

• 48 •

Blissful happiness
Enjoying togetherness
Sharing light talks
Throughout our life walks.

33. GOALS SET

Goals can be set
Devote energy
Efforts to achieve
All set in a row.

Selfish goals
Hard to enlist the support
Pessimist, egocentric
Discouraged, demotivated
Let them not dominate.

Try to ignore, focus
Forward march
Be patient
Try hard, ponder
On your dreams
With deals.
Believe in
Enthusiastic dedication
In whatever you
Were denied to do
For you to overcome and shine.

34. FEAR

To get to the top
Fear is the hurdle.
Fear within,

Fear of not accomplishing
The Impossible
Fear of being imperfect
Fear of challenges
Unwelcome, shut down
The fear, face it.
Never run away
Shudder not to face it.
For it would only
Shrink you within
Kill your initiative
innovation, enthusiasm.
Open the doors to challenges
Experience the thrilling
A game called LIFE-
Ocean of opportunities.

35. LIGHT

Let me be the light
That glows bright.
Let me be the light
That blows the night.
Let me be the light
That shows the way.
Let me be the light
That paves the path.
Let me be the light
That leads not to destruction.
Let me be the light
That spreads joy always.
Let me be the light
That greases the troubles
Let me be the light
That brightens the world
With the love I have in me.

36. TRAVELLING TRANSITION

Bumps, jumps, dumps
Holding onto the responsibilities
Shoulders let not them droop
And down you fall
Let them not be a showdown
No words, not a word
Should break you down
A showdown would be it
For those who
Toppled you down
Pained were the words
Let not those distorted

37. A TEACHER

Have you seen
Some well-dressed lady
Racing quickly down the street?
Have you seen
Some lady on a scooter
Riding hurriedly down the street?

Wondered who could that be.
So restless, so very careless!
Wondered who could that be.
Pleading with the traffic inspector!

Have you tried to send her
To olympics?
Had you ever caught her
Telling lies?
Have you been attending here
All through the years?
Had you ever thought her
To be your mentor?

Wondered what could be the rush.
So energetic, so very joyous!
Wondered who could it be.
Pleading with the students!

38. NOW DO YOU KNOW WHO SHE IS? CRY

It good to cry
To let that huge monster out.
That which fostered within you
That which swelled up as tears
That which cleansed ur eyes dry

That which could clean your sins
Sins of your forefathers
For the blood that runs
Through in you
Passes out what they saved for you

Thicker blood
Cleaned by the water
Swelling out as tears
May deliver us from Hither.

39. GRACE

Start to act instead of reacting.
Accept the change, let go.
Can't tread through spiritual path
To walk past others' choices.

Slow down the pace breathe in breathe out
Do not vent your anger.
Listen to your inner self
To not end up losing oneself.

Amend thy flaws truthfully
Start afresh, step away
Refrain from destructive ways
Step back, for blemish may smog
Thy walk through the world

To live up to grace.

40. REVELATION IN DESOLATION

I am tired,
of living life,
of living in strife.
of being undesired.

I am really tired,
of my burden of sins,
of hearing what conspired,
of throwing stuff in garbage bins.

I am extremely weary,
of being dreary,
of thinking about the past,
of feeling like an outcast.

I am done,
Being silent,
With being non-violent,
With having fun.

I am going to end it all.

I will hurt them all.
I will send them to hell,
I will rejoice in a final bell.

In sorrow's sea, I yearn to dive,
Absorb the tears in which we thrive.
To witness every tear shed,
Until no more can be bled.

I am going to rejoice,
In their shrieks.
I will mock their choice,
and call them freaks!

I will speak my mind,
I will stand my ground,
I will find my joy,
In all the misery around.

41. ECHOES OF THE VOID

Empty.
I have voided it all,
like a barren hall.
I have nothing to recall,
no misery to befall.
I have no one to call,
no voices in this squall.
I got no reason to play ball,
in this game where I always fall.

Alone.
I have it all in life.
No one to share my strife.
No voices in my head.
Left with a cold bed.

Death.
I am waiting for that,
like a cat looking for a pat.
It feels good,

as it changes my mood.

• •

Rage.
I just want to rage.
But I am in a cage,
a cage of consequence.
My conscience costs ten pence.

42. JOURNEY OF LIFE

My boat floats on this river,
Writhing as if in a fever.
I pass through a deserted town.
Which sends me into a frown.

I have been in that borough once.
Oh, wasn't it a bustling place of fun!
Had happiness there in tons.
A place kissed amply by the sun.

It's now a relic of the past,
which makes me sad.
I could have lived in that fad.
Oh, how life goes fast!

My boat floats on this river,
Like a car without a driver.
I pass through vast, lush plains.
It gives me guilt-laden pain.

I used to lie there and dream.
About a gentle stream.

Where I float paper boats
Amongst a family of stoats.

Now it's barren among the barren lands.
Lost in the vast ocean of cold sands.
I cry my heart out to moisten the turf.
All in vain as a snake claimed the turf.

My boat floats on this river,
Like death is its driver.
I reach a big, golden gate.
I feel a certain hate.

The gate was huge, hiding a great castle,
Unruffled by the deluge, built with no hassle.
I see a man in bed, all alone and sick.
With a small head, all sober with a stick.

That man had everything he wanted.
So much that even Lady Luck ranted.
But deep within he had no soul.
His past was utterly foul.

My boat floats on this river,
I let out a shiver.
I have seen all I could see.
I just want to be free.

My boat still floats on this river,
I will give my liver.
To get out of this damn river.
I feel my body quiver.

Such is the journey of life.
It is full of strife.
It is full of unfulfilled dreams.
All you are left with are angry screams.

43. PARTNER

My umbrella flew away
Must have But I did not want to.
Carried far away by the wind
Leaving me for some reason
Made me feel at ease.
Should have let it go earlier
In pursuit of
The love of my life.
The vacuum that it had created
Could not be filled till now
For the bond had not the space

To be filled by any other.
As that intimacy
Was never again
To be tasted.

www.ingramcontent.com/pod-product-compliance
Lightning Source LLC
Chambersburg PA
CBHW021133130726
47988CB00003B/1285